Iran and the West

Iran and the West

Philip Steele

rosen publishing's
rosen
central®

New York

Published in 2013 by The Rosen Publishing Group, Inc.
29 East 21st Street, New York, NY 10010

First Edition

Library of Congress Cataloging-in-Publication Data

Steele, Philip, 1948-
Iran and the West / Philip Steele.—1st ed.
     p. cm.—(Our world divided)
Includes bibliographical references and index.
ISBN 978-1-4488-6031-9 (library binding)
1. Iran—History—Juvenile literature. 2. Iran—Foreign relations—Juvenile literature.
I. Title.
DS254.75.S74 2012
955.06—dc23

                                                          2012010613

Manufactured in the United States of America

CPSIA Compliance Information: Batch #S12YA: For further information, contact Rosen Publishing, New York, New York, at 1-800-237-9932.

Contents

Chapter 1
Will this crisis go nuclear?   6

Chapter 2
The past—a key to the present   8

Chapter 3
Energy and security   14

Chapter 4
People and politics   22

Chapter 5
A religious state?   28

Chapter 6
Human rights   32

Chapter 7
Hopes for the future   38

Timeline   44

Glossary   45

For More Information   46

Index   47

Chapter 1
Will this crisis go nuclear?

Jet aircraft take off from runways in the desert, with an ear-splitting roar. Their vapor trails fill the skies. New missile and radar systems are placed in position and tested. Trucks full of heavily armed soldiers are put on standby.

This is not an actual war, but a military exercise being carried out over 232,000 square miles (600,000 square km) of Iranian territory in November 2010. The press calls such exercises "war games," but they are deadly serious. Their aim is to protect Iran's nuclear sites from future attack.

Is the risk of war a serious one? Some politicians in Israel and the United States of America have openly called for air attacks on Iran's nuclear sites. The Israeli airforce has also been practicing combat missions—in order to train for attacks upon Iran.

▲ *Troops of Iran's Revolutionary Guard test fire a Noor missile. This military exercise took place in southern Iran in April 2010.*

What is the problem?

The countries of the West (including the USA and its European allies) as well as Middle Eastern countries such as Israel, Saudi Arabia, and the Gulf states are worried that Iran is not just developing nuclear power, but nuclear weapons. They believe that this would be a major threat to world peace.

The government of Iran says that it has every right under international law to use nuclear power. It insists it has no intention of making or using nuclear weapons.

Divisions in world opinion are rarely straightforward. There are differences between the Western countries—and also within them—about this problem and how to deal with it. Within Iran itself the government has many opponents—but many of these are supportive of the country's nuclear program.

The bigger picture

This book will look more closely at the nuclear question. It will also study many other tensions that exist between Iran and the West. Western powers accuse Iran of supporting their enemies, including terrorist organizations. They see Iran as threatening Israel, a close ally of the United States. They also accuse the Iranian government of abusing basic human rights and of persecuting its opponents.

The Iranian government rejects all these accusations. It complains that the West is interfering in its internal affairs. It says that Westerners fail to understand Iran's religious and cultural traditions. It points out that Israel's occupation and settlement of Palestine are illegal under international law, and that the West ignores Israel's existing nuclear weapons, which threaten Iran.

This book questions the various arguments put forward by both sides, by journalists, campaigners, and politicians. It does not provide immediate answers, but it does aim to start a debate about important issues such as nuclear weapons, human rights, religion, and government. These are issues that affect people all over the world.

Before 1935, Iran was known as Persia. Just over half of the population today belong to the Persian ethnic group. Many minority groups also live in Iran, including Azeris, Kurds, Arabs, and Baluchis.

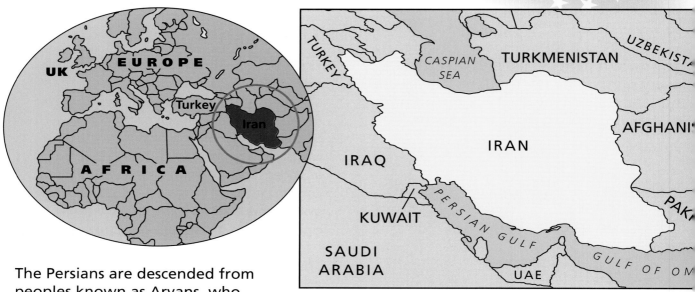

The Persians are descended from peoples known as Aryans, who began to migrate from southern Russia into the Middle East and India about 4,000 years ago. By 546 BCE the Persian empire stretched from Turkey to Pakistan.

▲ *Iran stretches from the shores of the Caspian Sea to the hot and humid Persian Gulf. Central flatlands are surrounded by high mountain ranges. The map on the left shows Iran's location on the world map.*

War and peace

Conflict is nothing new in this region. Many invading armies rode into Persia over the ages. The Arab invasion in 637 CE brought a new faith, called Islam. Most Persians came to follow the Shi'a branch of Islam. Shi'ite Muslims are a minority in the Islamic world, which is dominated by Sunni Muslims. Shi'ites hold different views about the family and descendants of the Prophet Muhammad, and about the role of the wider Muslim community.

Persia flourished as an independent nation in the 200s CE and in the 1600s. It lay on important overland trading routes between China, Western Asia, and Europe. Persian culture influenced much of Asia, and fascinated the distant Europeans.

Foreign empires

By the 1700s and 1800s European empire builders were competing with each other to win power and trade around the world. Overland trade through Persia grew less because European ships were now carrying goods from the Far East by sea. The Russian empire was moving into

Central Asia. Great Britain was winning control of India.

Many people see today's problems in this part of Asia as dating back to this period of overseas interference. The Iranian rulers of the day failed to stand up to foreign pressure, and gave away trading concessions. They were forced to withdraw these in 1890 after widespread protests. Muslim clerics and scholars united the opposition to Western intrusion. In 1907 a weakened Persia was divided into Russian and British areas of influence. The British soon struck oil. Oil offered vast riches, but it also brought political strife.

Rights were granted to the Anglo-Persian Oil Company, later part of BP. Persia received only 16 percent of the profits. During World War I (1914-18) British and Russian soldiers occupied Persia to secure their oil supplies.

New rulers

In 1921 an army officer called Reza Khan seized power in Persia with British support. He was declared Shah (king) in 1925 and ruled as a dictator. He set out to modernize the country, which he renamed Iran. His reforms of dress and traditional customs angered many muslims.

Viewpoints

"Our dear country, Iran, throughout history has been subject to threats."

Mahmoud Ahmadinejad

"I am Xerxes, great king, king of kings; the king of countries which speak all kinds of languages, the king of the entire, big, far-reaching Earth."

Xerxes I (Hsayarsa, 519-465 BCE)

▼ *Persia's rulers built splendid palaces at Susa and Persepolis.*

• Mahmoud Ahmadinejad has been President of Iran since 2005.

• Xerxes I was the ruler of the ancient Persian empire.

• Persia has an ancient history, which includes periods of great military power but also long periods of foreign domination. How might people's understanding of their national history affect their present ideas and actions?

Whose oil?

Russian (Soviet) and British troops also occupied Iran during World War II, staying from 1941 to 1946. The Western powers replaced the first Shah, whose sympathies lay with Nazi Germany, with his son Mohammad Reza Shah Pahlavi.

In 1951 Iran's democratically elected prime minister, Mohammad Mossadeq, brought in social reforms and nationalized Iranian oil. There was growing unrest and the new Shah was forced to flee the country. However the Western powers were determined to keep control of the oilfields. A coup was organized by the United States Central Intelligence Agency (CIA), with British support. Mossadeq was imprisoned. This attack on national sovereignty still angers many Iranians today. Reza Shah Pahlavi was restored to power and Western companies won back control of Iran's oil.

The USA and the Shah

Iran's links with the USA became stronger. The US provided aid and new technology. They wanted a strong anti-communist government in Iran to oppose neighboring communist Russia, which had become its enemy. This was during a period of global political tension, known as the Cold War (1945-89).

The Shah was ruthless in putting down communist or Muslim opposition to his rule. His secret police force, known as Savak, was founded in 1957 and was much feared. Savak agents were trained by the American CIA and by Mossad, the Israeli secret service.

Social reforms

In 1963 the Shah launched a "White Revolution," with the aim of improving agriculture and winning support from poor farmers. There was better, free education. Women gained the vote and had more

▲ *Women protest against the Shah in 1979. They point to the sky, saying that even patterns on the Moon represent the face of Iran's next leader, Ruhollah Khomeini.*

opportunities. However the reforms ended up creating more division than unity. Public funds were seen to be wasted on lavish royal spectacles. For Iran's Muslim clerics, life was becoming too Western and too secular.

The 1979 revolution

In 1975 the Shah made Iran a one-party state. Opponents were imprisoned or exiled. By 1979 the streets were increasingly filled with angry protestors—communists, republicans, liberals, and Muslim activists. Many of these activists held very traditional religious views and were known in the West as "fundamentalists." The Shah was overthrown and fled the country.

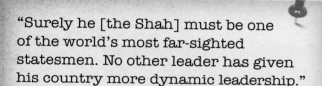

Viewpoints

"Surely he [the Shah] must be one of the world's most far-sighted statesmen. No other leader has given his country more dynamic leadership."

Margaret Thatcher, 1978

"Are we to be trampled underfoot by the boots of America simply because we are a weak nation and have no dollars?"

Ruhollah Khomeini, 1964

- Khomeini was an Islamic cleric and opponent of the Shah.

- Margaret Thatcher is a former British Prime Minister. She became prime minister in 1979.

- Today's confrontations were already shaping up in the 1960s and 70s, during the reign of the Shah. Was the West right to see the Shah as a force for stability in the Middle East, or did his rule lead to today's divisions?

▲ *The face of the new order. Portraits of the cleric Ruhollah Khomeini were held high at protests and rallies in and after 1979.*

Khomeini's Iran

The creator of the new Iranian state was Ruhollah Khomeini, a senior cleric. He is often referred to as the Ayatollah or Imam Khomeini. Although he had spent 14 years in exile, a crowd of six million Iranians greeted him on his return in 1979.

Khomeini was a longtime opponent of the Shah and the Western powers. He seized power as Supreme Leader, setting up an Islamic Republic based on strict religious observance. Other groups that had also opposed the Shah, such as democrats, communists, and rival Islamic groups, were banned. Many were imprisoned or executed, while others fled abroad.

Despite their sharp differences, in the 1980s the West secretly tried to seek favor with the Khomeini government with the hope of remaining a power in the region and having access to its oil. The West provided the new regime with weapons and supplied it with intelligence about communist activists within Iran. Even so, there were constant political crises between Iran and the West.

Troubled times

When the USA refused to return the former Shah for trial in Iran in 1979, 66 members of the US embassy staff in Tehran were seized and taken hostage by angry Khomeini supporters. The siege of the embassy lasted 444 days, during which a US rescue mission failed.

Neighboring Iraq attacked Iran in 1980. Iraq was in dispute with Iran over its border territory. It feared that the Islamic revolution would spread to its own Shi'ite Muslim minority. This war continued until 1988. Neither side won, but half a million people died. During the war, Iraqi dictator Saddam Hussein received support from the West. In 1988, missiles from a US aircraft carrier shot down an Iran Air civilian flight over the Persian Gulf, killing 290 passengers.

Human rights were also at the center of Iran's dispute with the West. In 1989 Khomeini pronounced a *fatwah* (a religious ruling) declaring that a novel by the British Indian novelist Salman Rushdie was blasphemous and that he should be killed. Rushdie was forced into hiding. There were anti-Rushdie protests by Muslims in many parts of the world, countered by Western calls for freedom of speech.

▲ *The US embassy hostages were released between 1979 and 1981.*

New directions

Khomeini died in 1989. He was followed as Supreme Leader by Ali Khamenei, who had until then been serving as president. Between 1989 and 1997 President Ali-Akbar Hashemi Rafsanjani started to bring in economic reforms.

Mohammad Khatami was elected president in 1997. He was a political reformist, who called for better foreign relations and improved human rights. This marked the beginning of a struggle between reform and religious tradition in Iran, which continues today.

Ahmadinejad and the opposition

The 2005 presidential election was won by Mahmoud Ahmadinejad. He was a fiery public speaker, an anti-Western conservative who aimed to increase Iran's regional power. Ahmadinejad was also declared winner of the 2009 presidential election, despite claims that the voting was rigged. Big street protests in support of the losing candidates became known as the "Green Revolution." The protests were put down harshly, with thousands of arrests and many deaths. Ahmadinejad accused the protestors of being backed by foreign interests.

▲ *Tehran is in the north of Iran.*

Iran today

Name: Islamic Republic of Iran

Capital: Tehran

Major cities: Esfahan, Tabriz, Shiraz, Mashhad, Ahvaz, Qom

Population: 76,923,300

Religions: Shi'a Islam 89 percent; Sunni Islam 9 percent; others 2 percent (Zoroastrianism, Judaism, Christianity, Bahai)

Average adult literacy: Men 84 percent; women 70 percent

Resources: Oil, natural gas, uranium

Chapter 3

Energy and security

Nearly a third of young Iranian school leavers can expect to work in industry, rather than on farms or in city offices. The country's biggest industry by far is the production and processing of oil and natural gas. These two fuels supply the power for over 93 percent of Iran's own electricity, and are the country's most important exports.

In fact, one half of the whole national budget depends on income from these fuels. Iran's oil and gas reserves are among the largest on Earth. They are mostly located in the west and south of the country, and offshore in the Persian Gulf.

Oil and politics

Iran already provides nearly 5 percent of the whole world's oil needs. Iran's oil riches give it bargaining power in world politics. It is also one reason why Iran has been at the center of political disputes for the last one hundred years.

▲ *The Iranian port of Asalouyeh serves the world's largest field of natural gas.*

Iran already sells a lot of its oil to fuel-hungry China, which has the world's fastest growing economy. As a result, Iran receives some political support from China.

Most of the world's oil dealings are paid for in US dollars. However as a result of the crisis in its relations with the USA, Iran decided in 2007 to use other currencies, such as the Euro, when trading its oil. This decision increased tension between the two countries. The location of regional oil and gas pipelines is another hot international issue. Iran's opponents try to find routes for international pipelines to Europe or India that bypass Iran.

Nuclear power?

Like many countries, Iran uses a small amount of renewable energy. It is also developing nuclear power. Nuclear sites include the Bushehr nuclear power station, in southwestern Iran on the coast of the Persian Gulf. This was completed with Russian engineers in 2010. Near Natanz, in Central Iran, there is a center for enriching uranium, a scientific process necessary for making nuclear fuel. At Fordu, near the city of Qom in Central Iran, there is another enrichment site, which was kept secret by Iran until 2009. Iran has its own uranium mines, and in 2010 announced the successful processing of the output.

▲ *Ahmadinejad defends Iran's nuclear program to the world media in 2006.*

Viewpoints

"Iranian President Mahmoud Ahmadinejad reiterated that international and unilateral sanctions against Iran will leave no negative impact on the country's progress, stressing that pressures will merely strengthen Tehran's resolve to move forward."

Fars News Agency report, Iran, October 2010

"India Starts Looking Beyond Iran for Oil ... Iran...has been increasingly isolated from its customers [including India] due to trade restrictions and sanctions aimed at slowing down its nuclear program..."

Gurdeep Singh, January 2011

• The first quote is from a news report in Iran.

• Gurdeep Singh is writing for the *Wall Street Journal*, a US paper based in New York.

• Trading restrictions or sanctions imposed on Iran by the USA do affect its oil industry—and therefore its whole economy—as well as its nuclear development. Do you think the current crisis is more about who controls Iran's oil than about nuclear weapons?

Nuclear power—or bombs?

There are many arguments against nuclear power. These concern expense, operating safety and the disposal of radioactive waste. However these are not the issues for which Western governments criticize Iran. Western governments and companies are themselves launching new civil nuclear power programs worldwide. Indeed, it was the United States that started off Iran's nuclear program in the 1950s, under the rule of the Shah, launching the Tehran Nuclear Research Center in 1967.

Iran is enriching uranium. It has the right to do this according to the international Nuclear Non-Proliferation Treaty (NPT), of which it is a member state. However under NPT rules, Iran is not allowed to enrich uranium to a grade suitable for making weapons. President Ahmadinejad and also Iran's religious leaders have insisted that Iran is opposed to all nuclear weapons and only interested in nuclear power.

Who do you believe?

However many Western politicians simply do not believe them. They say that Iran is planning to enrich uranium for making nuclear weapons. Some people say that Iran could already be capable of producing a nuclear bomb within two years, or even less. Western security experts are divided in their opinions.

Nuclear fission: war or peace?

• The center of an atom is called its nucleus. When two nuclei or particles are made to collide, a nuclear reaction takes place, which causes them to change their structure. This releases energy.

• Inside a nuclear reactor there are fuel rods made of the element called uranium. The uranium fuel must be enriched before it works properly in a reactor. When particles called neutrons are smashed into the uranium rods, the atoms split—a process called fission. The heat released is used to turn water into steam, which turns the turbines that generate electricity.

• Nuclear fission can also be used to create massive explosions. Nuclear bombs can devastate cities and whole regions in seconds. Many people die immediately. Others die over a longer period, having been made sick by radioactivity.

• The fuel used to make nuclear bombs must be enriched to a higher level than the uranium used in power stations. Until this stage is reached, it is not clear whether nuclear research is for energy production or war.

• Since its beginnings in the 1950s, nuclear power has been closely linked with the development of nuclear weapons.

Viewpoints

▲ *An Iranian Ghassed smart bomb during an Army Day parade in Tehran in 2009.*

"There is little doubt that Iran is on a mission to rebuild its nuclear weapons and use that capability to wreak havoc and destruction on Israel and others throughout the world."

Russ Carnahan, 2005

"We have not diverted from a peaceful path... There is a solution here, however, a very simple solution. The countries that have atomic bombs should destroy their stockpiles."

Mahmoud Ahmadinejad, 2007

• Russ Carnahan is a Democrat and a member of the US House of Representatives.

• The second quote is from President Ahmadinejad of Iran, as interviewed on CBS.

• Who can be believed? It is difficult to say. Iran has been repeatedly inspected by the International Atomic Energy Authority (IAEA), but no evidence of uranium being set aside for weapons grade enrichment has been found. A February 2010 IAEA report confirmed this, but did say that Iran had been uncooperative and that this raised concerns.

Sanctions against Iran

The Security Council of the United Nations (UN) has ordered Iran to stop all preparation and enrichment of uranium ore. Iran says that it has every right to carry out these activities. The UN has imposed four sets of sanctions on Iran, with the intention of limiting its nuclear development. The USA too has placed economic sanctions on Iran—ever since 1979—and the nations of the European Union (EU) also brought in sanctions in 2010.

The Western powers have offered to lift many sanctions and to provide fuel and other assistance for nuclear power stations, if Iran stops all uranium enrichment—but by 2011 no long-term agreement had been reached.

Secret attacks and cyber-war

Meanwhile there is a suggestion that secret direct action is being taken by Iran's opponents, in addition to sanctions. A computer worm known as Stuxnet, which affected Iran's enrichment process in 2010, was widely believed to be a cyber-attack by foreign powers. In the same year two Iranian nuclear physicists were assassinated, and a third wounded. In 2011 Iranian television broadcast the apparent confession of an Iranian to one of these attacks, saying that he was an agent working for Israel. Should not all countries operate with transparency rather than secrecy? Some would disagree, arguing that if the danger of Iranian nuclear weapons is real, extreme remedies are required.

Case Study

Shahram Amiri, a nuclear spy?

In the summer of 2009 an Iranian nuclear scientist named Shahram Amiri traveled to Mecca, in Saudi Arabia. What happened next? There are many different versions of this story. Iranian PressTV reported that Amiri had been kidnapped and taken to the USA. *The New York Times* said that Amiri had been working as a spy for the USA,

Shahram Amiri holds his son's hand as he flashes the victory sign upon arrival at Imam Khomeini Airport in Tehran, July 15, 2010.

and had been helped to escape by the CIA. People thought it might have been him who revealed the existence of the secret uranium enrichment site near Qom.

A year later Amiri turned up at the Pakistan embassy in Washington, DC, and asked to be returned to Iran. On arrival in Tehran he was given a hero's welcome. He claimed he had been drugged in Mecca and seized against his will by US agents and taken to the USA. Was Amiri really a double agent, working all along for Iran rather than the USA?

Or was he actually forced to return because his family had been threatened back in Iran? In January 2011 US news sources reported that the Iranian opposition believed Amiri was now in jail and being tortured. We may never know the truth of this case—but it does show the murky world of espionage (spying) and secrecy behind the scenes.

The nuclear threat

The proliferation or spread of nuclear weapons is one of the greatest threats to world security, especially in a region like the Middle East, which has many political problems and grievances. Nuclear material can be acquired by terrorists as well as by governments. A nuclear attack could have a huge death toll and devastate the environment.

The big powers, such as the USA, Russia, China, Britain, and France, already have nuclear weapons and are members of the NPT. What about other states in Western and Southern Asia? India, Pakistan, and Israel all have nuclear weapons with the support of the West, even though they have not signed up to the NPT. Israel refuses to allow any international inspection of its nuclear weapons.

Nuclear politics

The West's argument then is not a matter of opposition to any nuclear weapons as much as a matter of principle. It aims to prevent only those nations that may threaten its interests from having nuclear weapons, or those nations that are likely to use them. Isn't that reasonable? Surely, every country in the West has a legitimate duty to safeguard the security of its own citizens? But in that case doesn't Iran have the same right? Either side that used nuclear weapons, in attack or defense, would be putting world peace at risk—including the security of its own citizens.

Supporters of nuclear disarmament say that the only logical and just policy is to ban the development, holding or use of all nuclear weapons worldwide. Some opponents

▲ *An Iranian opposition supporter protests at the Place des Nations, December 2010, in Geneva as world powers hold a meeting with Iran over its disputed nuclear program.*

of nuclear power would say that if civil and military uses of nuclear fission are so closely linked, then both should be banned. Supporters of nuclear deterrence however believe that the possession of nuclear weapons by both sides in a global dispute can keep the peace, as neither side will risk complete destruction.

Iran's production of oil and its use of nuclear fuels are at the center of this crisis. But they are not the only reasons for current divisions and political tensions.

Viewpoints

"IAEA: Iran has over 2 tons enriched uranium—2 bombs' worth."

Headline, *Jerusalem Post*, January 2010

"Iran makes a second appearance at number eight, due to the media's obsession with the nuclear question, which President Ahmadinejad seems happy to goad."

Al Jazeera compares frequency of its headline topics in the year 2010

• Most of us rely on the communications media to find out news about Iran. How reliable are newspapers and broadcasts? Do media companies have their own agenda? Are they state-controlled, publishing propaganda or "spin," or are they independent? Do journalists ask searching questions? Coverage of the Iranian nuclear crisis on Fox News, CNN, BBC, Al Jazeera and Iran's PressTV may differ greatly. It can be compared on Internet sites such as You Tube.

"... there has been little in the way of Western media coverage or questioning whether this could in fact be a civilian [nuclear power] programme [in Iran]."

Greg Simons, *European Journalism Centre* online magazine, January 2010

▼ *Iran's chief negotiator Saeed Jalili at a press conference closing nuclear talks, December 2010, Geneva.*

Chapter 4

People and politics

I ran is a young country, with 22 percent of the population being under 14. Boys and girls have to go to school from 6 to 14, after which they may go on to high school, university, or a technical college. Life in the countryside is much more traditional than life in the modern cities. There are differences between the well off and the poor, and between varying religious outlooks.

Iranian society, like any other, contains differences between generations, between city and country folk, between social classes. It is the Iranian public who form opinion, who take part in the political system and are affected by its laws—and its international crises and foreign relations.

Iran's political system

The way in which any country is organized politically is shown in its constitution. A constitution lays out a nation's system of government, its laws and rights. It generally takes the form of a special document or bill, as in the United States and as in Iran. In the United Kingdom there is no written constitution, just the body of laws that have grown up over the ages. The UK is however

signed up to the European Convention on Human Rights. The Iranian constitution was voted in in 1979 and amended ten years later. It is unusual because it combines in one document some very different political ideas.

The state and religion

Iran is sometimes referred to as a theocracy, a country ruled by religious officials. Clerics certainly hold great political power. They sit on the influential Guardian Council. Islamic scholars make up the Assembly of Experts, which has the power to block parliamentary candidates and appoint or remove the most powerful politician in the land, the Supreme Leader. The power held by these clerics is not democratic.

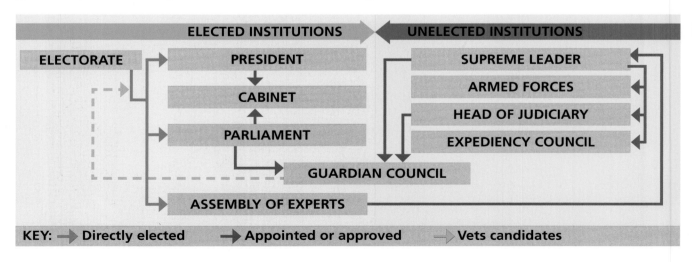

▲ *How it works—the mechanics of government in Iran.*

Power and money

Elections for the presidency and the Majlis, or parliament, are public and supposed to be democratic. Other aspects of the political system are authoritarian, such as the overriding powers of the assemblies and councils.

Another authoritarian element is the Revolutionary Guard. At the forefront of the 1979 Revolution, the Guards now form an increasingly powerful branch of the armed forces. They also run their own business empire, which has been targeted by Western economic sanctions. They are allied to a political street militia, the Basij.

The Iranian economy still includes a great deal of state ownership, with the government controlling many resources and businesses. For some years plans have been made to privatize the economy, in the belief that this will make it more efficient. As a result, the government's role in wealth creation (Gross Domestic Product or GDP) dropped from 80 percent in 2005 to 40 percent in 2009.

Viewpoints

"Soon after his election in 2005, President Ahmadinejad named several former [Revolutionary Guard] veterans to key ministries in his cabinet. After his disputed re-election in June [2009], the Revolutionary Guards warned demonstrators against further protests."

BBC News, October 2009

"Now the Revolutionary Guard is taking arms against the people, arresting opposition figures and stifling freedom of expression and imposing itself on the economy in an unbelievable way."

Mir-Hossein Mousavi, presidential candidate in 2009

• Mousavi, a veteran politician of the Khomeini years, opposes President Ahmadinejad's hard line and believes that the time has come for Iran to reform.

▶ *Members of Iran's Revolutionary Guard march during a 2007 parade to commemorate the Iran-Iraq War (1980-88).*

Ideals and the reality

Iran's constitution is one thing. How Iran is actually run from day to day, is another. Although the constitution contains assurances of protection for basic human rights, the government frequently ignores them.

International relations

Western countries are of course free to criticize the way in which other countries run their affairs. But do they have the right to actively interfere in the affairs of other nations, or even threaten them with war? Should it not be up to the people who live in those countries to accept or to change their government? For over two centuries the West has repeatedly intervened in the Middle East. Has it been serving its own interests rather than those of the people who live there? Have its policies been successful or counter-productive?

Similar questions should of course be asked of Iran. It has repeatedly interfered in the politics of neighboring Afghanistan and given support to Shi'a militias in Iraq. In Lebanon Iran has funded and supplied Hizbullah. This organization has resisted Israeli invasions of Lebanon and attacked Israeli territory with rockets. Iran has also supported Hamas, a Palestinian political party, whose military wing has carried out rocket and terrorist attacks on Israel. Hamas fairly won the 2006 Palestinian parliamentary election, but has been shunned by Western governments, who have declared both Hizbullah and Hamas to be terrorist organizations.

Iran points out in its turn that Israel breaks international law in settling occupied Palestinian territory and has abused the rights of Palestinians. Is US anger actually centered on Iran's policy towards Israel? Iran certainly wants to be the major regional power in the Middle East and this worries the West as well as some neighboring countries. Some fear that fundamentalism in its Iranian form will take root in their own countries and threaten their power.

◄ *Iran supports Hamas and Hizbullah. Here Palestinian Hamas militants, dressed as suicide bombers, take part in a rally in Gaza, 2010.*

Viewpoints

"Speaking in the US Senate... [Hillary] Clinton announced that Washington had asked Syria to 'begin to move away from the relationship with Iran, which is so deeply troubling to the region as well as to the United States.'"

"During their meeting, the Iranian and Syrian presidents delivered harsh responses to Clinton's comments... Assad expressed strong support for the Islamic Republic of Iran, saying the US stance toward Iran is another instance of colonialism in the region."

The Tehran Times, February 2010 (both)

• Both of these quotes are reports from *The Tehran Times* in 2010 and show the official view of the US and the view of the Iranian and Syrian presidents.

• The USA is trying to limit Iranian influence across the region and Syria is seen as a key player.

• Consider why each public figure might feel as they do about Iran and Syria.

Iran's President Ahmadinejad shakes hands with Syrian President Bashar al-Assad, October 2010 in Tehran.

US diplomacy

After Barack Obama became president in 2009, the USA tried a more diplomatic approach towards Iran than it had during the presidency of George W. Bush (2001-09). Bush had described Iran as being part of an "axis of evil." However, Ahmadinejad has not eased his opposition to the USA. Obama has stepped up economic sanctions while avoiding war.

Opposition and dissent

At home Ahmadinejad's policies are just as controversial. He was accused by many Iranians of voter fraud and intimidation during the 2009 presidential elections. Ahmadinejad claimed that the "Green Revolution" protests were being stirred up by foreign agents. The CIA is certainly active within Iran, and Iranian exiles also maintain links with their families and friends who remain in Iran. However independently of overseas bodies, there is a growing opposition within Iran. The electronic media, despite censorship, have made it easier for this movement to organize.

There is clearly widespread support for change and reform, even within the existing political structure. The changes opponents are calling for include further economic reform, improved human

▲ *Supporters of Mousavi wave green flags at a pro-reform rally in Tehran in 2009.*

rights and personal freedoms, and more democratic politics. A wide range of political programs is found amongst the many banned Iranian parties, which are exiled overseas.

The full spectrum of Iranian politics, taking in all social classes, ethnic groups, and various religious positions, including fundamentalist Islam, would of course include conservative, liberal, or radical elements. The West may be encouraging opposition at the moment, but it is by no means certain that a freely elected and fully democratic government would end up being pro-Western or would not aim to dominate the region.

A New Greeting to the World

Case Study

Mahmoud Ahmadinejad— man of controversy

Mahmoud Ahmadinejad was born in 1956. He studied engineering and went on to become Mayor of Tehran in 2003. He won the presidency in 2005 as head of a conservative coalition. Some critics of Iran have blamed the current divisions on the aggressive, individual style of politics favored by President Ahmadinejad. In foreign affairs he has taken each crisis to the brink, enjoying confrontation and controversy.

His dismissive comments about the Holocaust, the mass-murder of Jews by the German Nazis in the 1930s and '40s, have caused great offense. He has been accused of being anti-Jewish. He rejects this, saying that he is against Zionism (Jewish nationalism) and the Israeli government, but not the Jewish people. Some say that Ahmadinejad's views have been misrepresented or wrongly translated in the Western media. Whatever the truth, he has certainly inflamed feelings.

The Iranian president has also offended the US by suggesting that people within the United States government may have been behind the attack of "9-11" (September 11, 2001, when New York City's World Trade Center and other US targets were attacked with horrific loss of life by 19 terrorists, mostly Saudi Arabians).

Chapter 5

A religious state?

I ran's description of itself as an Islamic republic is an accurate reflection of the religious beliefs of most people in the country. Young people In Iran learn the holy scriptures of the Quran and are taught to honor the principles (or "pillars") of Islam, such as the importance of prayer, fasting, and charity. Ninety-nine percent of all Iranians are Muslims.

Of these, 95 percent belong to the Shi'a branch of the faith. Only 4 percent belong to the Sunni branch of Islam.

Religion and politics

Many discussions about relations between Iran and the West center upon religious beliefs and attitudes. One nation's religious beliefs are chiefly a matter for itself alone, and surely it is unwise for politicians of one religion to pass judgement on another faith. However if a religion is a formal part of a nation's political system, it inevitably becomes part of the debate about government policies.

Although Iran's Muslim clerics still influence almost all aspects of government policy, they do not hold a single political position. They include conservatives, but also opponents of the current government. The popular reformist Mohammad Khatami, who served as president from 1997 to 2005, was a liberal cleric. Equally devout Iranian Muslims may be supporters or opponents of the current government.

Many Western nations are critical of religion playing a major part in government. The US constitution, for example, forbids religion having an official role in the affairs of state. Even so, Christianity does play a big part in US political campaigning. In England and

▲ *Muslim clerics attend a rally in 1993 to commemorate the 1979 revolution.*

Scotland there are official or established Christian Churches—although their political role is very limited, and there is a strong secular (non-religious) element in public opinion.

Conflict or understanding?

There are religious people on all sides of the Iran-West divide—Christians, Muslims, and Jews—who regard the principles of their own faith as incompatible with those of other religions. They emphasise the differences between the faiths and believe that these play a part in the political crisis between the West and the Middle East as a whole.

Mutual mistrust and even religious hatred has been inflamed by acts of terrorism carried out in the name of Islam, as it has by wars carried out by Christian and Jewish armies against Muslim nations. There is certainly a long history of conflict between Christianity, Judaism, and Islam.

Viewpoints

"The Islamic Republic is a system based on belief in ... divine revelation and its fundamental role in setting forth the laws."

Constitution of Iran, Article 2 [ii]

"Congress shall make no law respecting an establishment of religion..."

United States Bill of Rights, 1st Amendment

▼ *The beautiful Shah Mosque in Esfahan.*

• The Iranian constitution bases government on religious faith. The constitutions of many Western countries, including the USA, separate religion from functions of the state.

• Think about how these different opinions on religion might affect the way a country is governed and the laws of a state.

Common ground

However there have also been historical periods of cooperation and understanding between the three faiths, which have existed alongside each other for so many centuries. These religions share a great deal. They all developed in Western Asia. Their believers all follow a single God, and honor many of the same religious figures, such as Abraham and Isaac. They share customs, tradition, and scholarship. Their ideals are intended to be based on peace.

Shari'a law

Most religions have special laws, based on scripture or teachings, which lay out a code of practice or morality. Sometimes these laws list punishments, which should apply to those who break them. Islamic law is called Shari'a. It is revered by all Muslims, but has been interpreted in various and very different ways.

In Iran conservative clerics have made a very harsh interpretation of Shari'a the basis of everyday civil or criminal law. Ancient punishments such as lashing or, more rarely, stoning have been revived, which conflict with basic human rights as agreed by the United Nations. Many Muslims in Iran and elsewhere do not approve of such punishments, which are universally condemned in the West.

Religious attitudes

Some Western politicians condemn Islamic "extremism" or "fundamentalism" as the root of problems across the Middle East.

▲ *At a rally in Berlin, the German capital, opponents of the Iranian government draw attention to the extreme cruelty of stoning.*

Case Study

Sakineh Ashtiani—condemned by religious laws

Sakineh Mohammadi Ashtiani is an Iranian woman of the Azeri ethnic group. She was born in 1967. In 2006 in Tabriz, she pleaded guilty, apparently after torture, to a charge of adultery (sex outside marriage) with two men. She received 99 lashes. Adultery is not illegal in most Western countries. Sakineh was later re-tried, with added charges of murder, and sentenced to death by stoning. The case received publicity around the world. In late 2010 it was announced that Sakineh would not be stoned, but people were still uncertain of her fate. Might she still be hanged? Would she be spared? There were accusations of forced confession, further cruel punishment and intimidation of her lawyers. The details of Sakineh's case have become confused amidst conflicting accusations but Sakineh's years in prison have certainly been a terrifying ordeal.

▲ *A portrait of Sakineh is unfurled at a protest in Rome.*

Some Muslim leaders condemn Western materialism and the lack of spiritual values in public life, as indeed do some Western Christians. Is radical Islam a purely spiritual movement or has it been influenced by social or political factors? Some link its rise with non-religious factors such as poverty, or the lack of a political voice. Some even see "fundamentalism" as a response to the West's own policies in the Middle East. The Western powers have repeatedly overthrown secular governments in the region if these were nationalist (for example wanting to take control of their own country's resources) or if they were communist.

The West even went as far as funding some religious fundamentalists in Iran as early as the 1950s. They also funded religious groups in neighboring Afghanistan in the 1980s, because these were fighting against the Russians. Such groups later gave birth to the Taliban movement, which has fought against the West in that country since 2001.

Chapter 6
Human rights

Iran has a very poor record when it comes to human rights. Human rights are those basic needs that have to be met if people are to lead a decent life and to be treated fairly. They may include liberty, equality, justice, health, education, security, political or religious freedoms, freedom to travel or freedom of speech.

The Universal Declaration

In 1948 the United Nations drew up guidelines called the Universal Declaration of Human Rights (UDHR). Universal means that this document applies to all people, nations and territories in the world, in all situations. The UDHR is not binding under international law, and is not fully observed by many member states of the UN. However it has been used as a basis for drawing up international conventions that do have legal effect, in areas such as the prevention of genocide, torture, racism, child protection, or discrimination against women.

The United Nations, the United States and the European Union have all criticized the government of President Ahmadinejad for many abuses of human rights in Iran. These complaints form part of the current grievances between the two sides.

Ahmadinejad rejects criticism by saying that many human rights in question are culturally Western and not universal, or that campaigns about rights are political plots by Iran's enemies.

Viewpoints

"Today we are moving from just criticizing the [Iranian] government ... to calling out individuals within the government whom we believe can be traced to abuses [of human rights]."

Hillary Clinton, US Secretary of State, September 2010

"Iran sentenced a prominent human rights lawyer to 11 years in prison on Sunday, highlighting an intensifying crackdown on lawyers that appears focused on people connected with 2003 Nobel Peace Prize winner Shirin Ebadi [see page 34]. The court also ruled that the lawyer, 47-year-old Nasrin Sotoudeh, is not allowed to practice law or leave the country for the next 20 years, her husband, Reza Khandan, said."

Thomas Erdbrink, *Washington Post Foreign Service*, January 2011

Execution and imprisonment in Iran

Independent human rights activists and international organizations strongly condemn the Iranian government. One major concern is capital punishment, which is banned in 95 of the world's nations and rarely or never used in a further 44. Iran is believed to have used the death penalty at least 388 times in 2009, a figure second only to China's and nearly eight times that of the USA. The death penalty is not just reserved for murder, but also applies to political crimes, drug offenses, and even homosexuality and adultery.

Rights activists are concerned by the imprisonment and execution of juveniles—people who committed the offense in question when they were under the age of 18. Iranian law sets the age of criminal responsibility at traditional dates for "adulthood"—about 15 for boys and only 9 for girls.

STOP KILLING IN IRAN !

• In 2010 US Secretary of State Hillary Clinton introduced economic sanctions against individual Iranian officials believed to have abused human rights. How effective do you think such policies are?

▲ *Overseas protestors focus on Iran's use of the death penalty.*

Punishments

The normal method of execution in Iran is hanging. Stoning to death may be the penalty for adultery. Stoning—throwing small stones at prisoners part-buried in the ground until they die—is a cruel and slow form of execution introduced in 1983. It is believed that six people were killed by stoning between 2006 and 2010. Unusually harsh corporal punishments include severe lashings.

▲ *A crowd of supporters greets Shirin Ebadi, a feminist lawyer, human rights activist, and 2003 winner of the Nobel Peace Prize.*

Iranian women

Western criticisms of Iran often focus upon the position of women in society. Although women are educated, forming a majority of university students, Iranian men receive favorable treatment according to traditional custom, under the law and in sentencing by the courts. This is the case in laws regarding rape and adultery and in the use of *siqeh*, a temporary marriage arrangement. In a court of law, a woman's evidence is regarded as less valid than that of a man. Women's rights have been a contentious issue between conservative and reformist Muslims in Iran.

In public places, women are expected to wear an Iranian version of Islamic dress, in dark colors, covering every part of the body except the hands and the open face. Many Muslim women feel that such dress is modest, proper, and practical. However many others would prefer to dress more freely, and particularly resent having to cover their hair. Policing of dress codes on the street is often rough, with harsh punishments.

Political rights

The Iranian government cracks down on political freedoms in the name of security. Secular, democratic, or radical political parties are banned. Many of them operate in exile. Political protests or gatherings are suppressed. Detention, illegal imprisonment, and unofficial torture take place.

Freedom of belief?

In most Western countries, religious minorities are allowed to worship freely and people have the right to be atheists. In Iran three religious minorities are recognized and given freedom of worship. These are Christians, Jews, and Zoroastrians, who follow a religion that dates back to ancient Persia. These three groups have separate political representation but restricted civil rights. Atheism and conversion to another religion from Islam is forbidden. Members of the Baha'i faith as well as some Islamic groups, such as Sufis and Ismailis, have suffered persecution in Iran since long before 1979. Many Iranian Jews have emigrated to Israel or the USA.

Viewpoints

"Everyone has the right to freedom of opinion and expression; this right includes freedom to hold opinions without interference and to seek, receive and impart information and ideas through any media and regardless of frontiers."

UN Universal Declaration of Human Rights, Article 19

"Publications and the press have freedom of expression except when it is detrimental to the fundamental principles of Islam or the rights of the public."

Constitution of Iran, Article 24

• The constitution of Iran places religious and political limits on freedom of expression.

• Jafar Panahi (b.1960) is an internationally acclaimed Iranian film-maker. In 2010 he was accused of making a film without permission and of calling for protests after the 2009 presidential election.

▼ *Iranian women attend a rally to mark International Women's Day, March 2004. Several hundred gathered despite the authorities claiming that it was illegal.*

"Mr Panahi has been sentenced to six years in jail on a charge of [taking part] in a gathering and carrying out propaganda against the system. He has also been banned from making films, writing any kind of scripts, travelling abroad and talking to local and foreign media for 20 years."

Farideh Gheirat, lawyer representing Iranian film-maker Jafar Panahi, December 2010

Minorities in Iran

Minority ethnic groups, especially the Kurds (who belong to the Sunni branch of Islam) have also been denied basic rights, with some held—or executed—as political prisoners. The Azeri people living in Iran complain that their language is banned in schools and that Azeri place names are changed to Persian.

Censorship and free speech

Censorship of the media was strict under Khomeini, but began to be relaxed by the reformist government of Khatami. Since Ahmadinejad came to power in 2005, freedom of speech has come under attack again, both from the government and from religious organizations. The government censors access to the Internet, books, newspapers and magazines, television and radio, art and exhibitions.

International comparisons

How does Iran's human rights record compare with that of other lands? Activists accuse many other states in the Middle East of human rights abuses, whether these countries are allies or opponents of the West. Saudi Arabia is criticized on the grounds of cruel and excessive punishments, lack of women's rights, as well as religious and political freedoms. Israel is criticized for the inequality of civil rights for its Arab citizens, and for its abuse of a wide range of basic rights for Palestinians in the territories of the West Bank and Gaza.

The Western nations, which did so much to bring about the United Nations human rights declaration, have themselves been accused of human rights abuses in the Middle East in recent years. The US-led wars in Afghanistan (from 2001) and Iraq (from 2003) led to accusations that the West had condoned torture and prisoner abuse. The kidnapping and detention without trial of suspects in the US base at Guantánamo Bay, on the island of Cuba, has been widely criticized.

Case Study

Zanan magazine

▲ **Banned**—Zanan *magazine, a favorite with Iranian women.*

Zanan means "woman" in Persian. It was the name of a popular independent magazine first published in Iran in February 1992 and edited by Shahla Sherkat. For 152 monthly issues over 16 years Zanan reported on women's issues, health, legal matters,

Human rights organizations believe that such policies have weakened the ability of Western governments to criticize others. They complain that during international negotiations or policy-making, Western governments are inconsistent. They may raise human rights issues when it suits their political purposes, but be ready to push them down the agenda, in order to win political or economic advantage.

Human rights activists from the West do sometimes underestimate the strength of cultural or religious customs, or misunderstand them. Is it realistic to expect views that took hundreds of years to develop in one part of the world to be accepted overnight in another?

leisure, arts, cinema, as well as news and international affairs. *Zanan* survived financial difficulties and political hostility, but was finally closed down in 2008 by the Press Supervisory Board, with the support of the Ministry of Culture and Islamic Guidance. They claimed it painted a dark picture of the Islamic Republic and published "morally questionable" articles.

◀ *Zanan's founder, Shahla Sherkat.*

Chapter 7

Hopes for the future

The solving of international crises is called conflict resolution. What is the way forward in Iran?

Can war solve the problem?

Some politicians in the West and Israel believe that military intervention in Iran presents less risk to world peace than a nuclear-armed Iran. If the West went to war with Iran might it not bring an end to this international crisis?

Opponents of this action point out that it would be in breach of international law, as long as Iran itself has not yet been shown to have actually produced any nuclear weapons. They also believe that military action would unite a majority of the Iranian people against the West, strengthening the power of conservative politicians such as Mahmoud Ahmadinejad.

The prospects of war are always very serious. This is particularly true in the Middle East, which is already being torn apart by long, brutal conflicts. Many military experts believe that a war in Iran would be even more devastating than the wars in Iraq and Afghanistan. Iran is a major military power and heavily armed. The loss of life would be high. The use of nuclear weapons in attack or defense, or the bombing of nuclear sites, would risk a massive environmental disaster, the lives of countless civilians and the risk of global nuclear warfare.

Critics of military action also warn that any new conflict could create political

Viewpoints

"Today, America is the number one enemy of our whole nation."

Ayatollah Ruhollah Khomeini, Supreme Leader of Iran 1979-89

"Trust can slowly be developed once again. We can contribute to this by moderating our tone ... A policy of detente [easing of tensions] will be a central issue for me."

Mir-Hossein Mousavi, *Der Spiegel*, April 27, 2009

- Khomeini was a conservative religious leader in the '70s and '80s.

- Mousavi is an Iranian reformist politician quoted in a German news source.

- Many politicians in Iran believe that the future lies not in confrontation, but in building up trust between opposing nations.

chaos and violence across the whole region. It could lead to a rise in international terrorism, rather than a decline. It could also create a worldwide energy crisis, because so much of the world's oil and gas comes from the Middle East. Might the effect of a war produce exactly the opposite result to the one intended?

Cyber-war—electronic attacks on the computer systems, which operate nuclear sites—is a non-violent alternative. However if such tactics and counter-attacks were to spread, they could paralyze computer systems around the world.

Economic pressure

The current economic sanctions are seen as the most appropriate policy by many Western governments. However wider or more severe economic sanctions, which may be more effective, can bring poverty and hardship to innocent citizens, as happened in the years before the invasion of Iraq in 2003. This could turn ordinary people against those countries imposing the sanctions.

The political situation in Iran would certainly change if a new reformist government were to be elected, with plans to improve human rights and foreign relations. This would reduce international tension. However under the present constitution, or with authoritarian parties being in control, what chance is there of any government being allowed to take office that reflects the genuine choice of all Iranians?

▲ *Campaigners march through London in 2007. They support all nuclear disarmament and oppose any war against Iran.*

Building bridges

Successful conflict resolution depends on diplomacy, on talking, exchanging information, and building up trust between individual politicians and, if possible, increased understanding by groups of ordinary citizens on both sides. Bridge-building has to be the first option, even if that is a very slow process. Politicians on both sides may find that patience gains them fewer favorable headlines in the press than calling for military threats or urgent confrontation.

But without diplomacy there can never be a long-term solution. Small practical steps need to be taken before major agreements can be reached. Diplomats

▲ *Iranian students call for democracy at Tehran University in December 2008.*

have to deal in real situations as they find them, and this almost always involves compromise.

Straight talking should also have its place in international relations. Double standards may weaken a country's bargaining power. It is pointless for Iran to point at the human rights listed in its constitution if these are not observed in practice, if political opponents are locked up or executed, or if women are stoned to death for adultery.

It is difficult for the Western nuclear states to prevent the spread of nuclear weapons on principle, if they then allow some nations in the region to have them, but others not. It is difficult to criticize one country for its human rights abuses, but to ignore similar abuses nearer to home. As soon as there is evidence of human rights abuse by any one nation, the international community must investigate the situation and take action. However it is pointless to remedy one injustice with another. The framework of international law needs to be honored and developed further if future conflict is to be avoided.

The wider world

The problem of Iran's relations with the West cannot be dealt with in isolation from the rest of the Middle East, which shares the same troubled history. There is a linkage of problems all the way across the African and Asian continent, from Egypt, Libya, Israel, Palestine, and Lebanon, through Iraq, Iran, Afghanistan, and Pakistan, southwards across the Arabian peninsula, north into Turkey, Russia, and Central Asia, eastwards to the borders of China. The peace of the whole world depends on the resolution of many conflicts in the region, not just one. In this the United Nations has the key role to play.

However in the end, it is up to the ordinary people of Iran to decide how they wish to go forward. The long history of the Iranian people has seen many great achievements and civilizations, as well as many crises and setbacks. The Iranians have proved that they are a resilient people, which should encourage all our hopes for the future.

▶ *US President Obama speaks out on Iran in Pittsburgh in 2009.*

What's to be done?

If these problems have vexed the most powerful countries in the world for two centuries, what can individuals do to help bring peace?

One thing they can do is to find out more about ordinary people who live on both sides of any political divide. How do they live from day to day? What do they enjoy? Find out about their home life, their food, what jobs they would like to do as adults. What do they learn at school or college? What are their personal religious beliefs, and how do they worship? People from different lands may find that they have much more in common than they had realized. They may also discover that ordinary people do not always hold the same views as their governments.

Viewpoints

"We have to prepare for the worst. The worst is war."

Bernard Kouchner, September 2007

"I think we need people to lower the rhetoric [persuasive language].... Everybody will benefit from a political settlement of the Iranian issue."

Mohamed ElBaradei

• Bernard Kouchner was the French Foreign Minister in 2007.

• Mohamed ElBaradei is the former chief nuclear inspector for the United Nations.

• War or political settlement? The politics of the Middle East affect the whole world. What do you think is the best way forward?

We all need to find out more about the history and the politics behind any international dispute. Books, Web sites, and newspapers can all help us to understand complicated issues. The Internet will provide comments on Iran from all sorts of organizations and individuals, from exiled political parties, from Iranian or other government sources, from people calling for war to others calling for peace. Which Web sites seem the most reliable?

Finally, young people who have a strong interest in issues such as human rights, the environment or international affairs can join campaigning groups or write to the press—remembering that in many parts of the world they might not have the freedom to take that action.

▼ *Children from Fars province in Iran.*

Timeline

1800s Persian rulers lose territory and trade to Russia and Britain. Mass protests.

1901 Britain wins rights to Persian oil reserves.

1907 Persia divided into British and Russian "spheres of influence."

1909 The Anglo-Persian Oil Company (APOC) is founded.

1911 Parliament overthrown by royal government, backed by Russians.

1914-18 World War I. British and Russian troops occupy Iran to secure oil supply.

1921 Army officer Reza Khan takes power in British-organized coup. Crowned as Shah (king) in 1925.

1935 Persia is renamed Iran. Islamic dress banned. Enforced "Westernization."

1939–45 World War II. British and Russian (Soviet) troops in occupation 1941–46.

1941 Reza is removed from rule by the British and Russians and replaced as Shah by his son Mohammad Reza.

1950 Nationalist Mohammad Mossadeq becomes prime minister.

1951 Oil is nationalized. British blockade oil exports.

1953 Shah forced to flee Iran. British and Americans overthrow Mossadeq. Shah returns.

1957 Savak secret police formed, trained by USA and Israel.

1963 White Revolution declared by Shah. Reforms opposed by clerics such as Ruhollah Khomeini, who is jailed.

1964 Americans in Iran exempted from Iranian law.

1967 US backs Iranian nuclear power program, opening of the Tehran Nuclear Research Center.

1975 Shah makes Iran a single-party state.

1978 Anti-Shah protests, hundreds killed.

1979 Shah flees Iran, dies in Egypt.

1980 Khomeini returns from exile. The Islamic Revolution. Opposition suppressed. Khomeini becomes Supreme Leader. Hostages taken at US embassy in Tehran (released 1981).

1980-88 Abolhasan Bani-Sadr first president. Iran-Iraq War. US ship shoots down Iran Air civilian flight.

1981 Iran resumes nuclear power program.

1989 *Fatwah* against author Salman Rushdie. Death of Khomeini. Replaced as Supreme Leader by Ali Khamenei. Ali-Akbar Rafsanjani becomes president.

1995 New US sanctions against Iran.

1997 Mohammad Khatami, a liberal reformist, becomes president.

1999 Pro-democracy student protests in Tehran.

2002 Russian engineers recommence work on the Bushehr nuclear reactor. US President George W. Bush says Iran is part of an "axis of evil."

2005 Mahmoud Ahmadinejad elected president. Increasing clampdown on opposition and human rights abuses.

2007 New US sanctions against Iran.

2009 Disputed election returns Ahmadinejad to power. Widespread protests by opposition.

2010 The Bushehr nuclear plant receives first fuel.

New US and UN sanctions against Iran.

International conference in Geneva on Iran's nuclear program, to be resumed in Istanbul January 2011.

Glossary

agenda A list of proposals to be discussed and acted upon.

atheist Not believing in God.

Ayatollah The name sometimes given to high-ranking clerics who are experts in Islamic studies.

blasphemous Offending or denying religious beliefs.

capital punishment The death penalty.

censorship The prevention of free expression or communication.

cleric A priest or religious official.

coalition An alliance of political parties.

colonialism The establishment of rule over a territory by people of another territory.

communist A political movement intended to give power to the working class and state control of the economy.

conservative Someone opposed to reform, a traditionalist.

corporal punishment Physical punishment involving pain.

coup A sudden seizure of political power, often by force.

diplomacy Discussing and making agreements between nations.

ethnic group Any group of people who share the same descent, customs, or language.

exile Being expelled from one's own country.

fatwah An opinion or ruling on an aspect of Islamic law issued by a Muslim scholar.

genocide The mass murder of a whole people because of their ethnicity.

Gulf states The nations bordering the Persian Gulf.

Holocaust The mass murder of millions of Jews, Roma, homosexuals, disabled people, and political opponents by German Nazis in Europe in WWII.

liberal In favor of progressive political reform.

Majlis The Iranian parliament.

materialism A way of living that is not centered on spiritual values.

minority A group of people smaller in number than a majority, perhaps in terms of their ethnic background or religion.

nationalize To place a business or a resource under state control.

nuclear deterrence The belief that possessing nuclear weapons puts off or deters other nations from using such weapons.

nuclear disarmament Getting rid of nuclear weapons.

nuclear power Electricity generated in a power station using nuclear fission.

nuclear weapons Nuclear bombs or rocket warheads that create massive explosions.

one-party state A country in which only one political party is allowed.

privatize To place a state-run industry or service under the control of a private company.

proliferation Spreading or increasing in number.

radar system An electronic system used to detect and locate objects such as aircraft or missiles.

reformist Seeking political reform.

republican Supporting government by the people.

reserves The amount of a valuable mineral, such as oil or coal, that is still in the ground.

sanction A measure taken, such as a blocking of trade, in order to punish a country for its policies.

Security Council The highest body within the United Nations (UN).

Shah The Persian term for a king.

Shari'a The religious law and practices of Islam. In some countries Shari'a forms the basis of civil law.

Soviet 1) A workers' council in a communist state 2) a citizen of the Soviet Union (1922-1991).

theocracy Any state in which clerics claim a God-given right to govern and draw up laws.

For More Information

Books

Changing Worlds: Iran by Richard Darqie (Franklin Watts, 2008)

Discover Countries: Iran by Rosie Wilson (Wayland, 2011)

Global Connections: Teens in Iran by David Seidman, Faeqheh Shiarazi and Alexa Sandmann (Compass Point Books, 2007)

Web Sites

Due to the changing nature of Internet links, Rosen Publishing has developed an online list of Web sites related to the subject of this book. This site is updated regularly. Please use this link to access the list:

http://www.rosenlinks.com/OWD/Iran

Index

Numbers in **bold** refer to illustrations.

Afghanistan **8**, 24, 31, 36, 38, 41
Ahmadinejad, Mahmoud 9, 13, 15, **15**, 16, 17, 21, 23, 25, **25**, 26, 27, 32, 36, 38, 45

China 8, 14, 20, 33, 41
CIA 10, 19, 26

democracy 22, 23, 26, 27, 34, 40, **40**, 45

Europe 7, 8, **8**, 15
European Union 18, 32

Great Britain **8**, 9, 10, 20, 22, 28–9, 45

human rights 7, 10, 12, 13, 22, 24, 26–7, 30, **30**, 31, **31**, 32–7, **33**, **34**, **35**, **37**, 39, 40, 41, 43

India 9, 15, 20
Iran 6, 7, 8, **8**, 9, 10, 11, 12, 13, 14, 15, **15**, 16, 17, 18, 19, 20, 21, 22, 23, 24, 25, 26, 27, 28, 29, 30, 31, 32, 33, 34, 35, 36, 38, 39, 40, 41, 42, **42–3**, 43, 44, 45
Iraq **8**, 12, **23**, 24, 36, 38, 39, 41, 45
Israel 6, 7, 17, 18, 24, 34, 36, 38, 41, 44

Khomeini, Ruhollah 10, **10**, 11, **11**, 12, 23, 36, 38, 45

Lebanon 24, 41

Muslims 8, 9, 10, 11, 12, 28, **28**, 29, 30, 34, 36, 44
  Shi'ite 8, 12, 13, 28
  Sunni 8, 13, 28, 36

natural gas 13, 14–15, **14**, 39
nuclear
  power 7, 15, 16, 18, 20, **20**, 21, **21**, **29**, 30, 36, 39, 44, 45
  war 6
  weapons 6, **6–7**, 7, 15, 16, 17, **17**, 18, 19, 20, 38, 39, 40–1, 44

oil 9, 10, 12, 13, **14–15**, 20, 39, 45

Pakistan 8, **8**, 19, 20, 41
Palestine 7, 24, **24**, 41
Persia 8, 9, **9**, 45

religion 7, 8, 11, 12, 13, 27, 28–31, **29**, 34, 36, 37, 44
Revolutionary Guard 23, **23**
Russia 8, 9, 10, 15, 31, 41, 45

sanctions 18, 26, 33, 39, 44, 45
Saudi Arabia 7, **8**, 18, 27, 36
Syria 25, **25**

Tehran 13, **13**, 19, **18–19**, **26–7**, 27, 45

United Nations 18, 30, 32, 35, 36, 41, 42, 44, 45

USA 6, 7, 10, 11, 12, 14, 15, 16, 17, 18, 19, 20, 22, 24, 25, 26, 27, 28, 29, 32, 33, 34, 36, 38, 41, **41**, 44
  embassy siege 12, **12**, 45

47

Photo Credits: The author and publisher would like to thank the following for allowing their pictures to be reproduced in this publication: Cover: Shutterstock/ Artography (top) and Henghameh Fahimi/AFP/ Getty Images; AFP/Getty Images: 40; Ahmad/Xinhua Press/Corbis: 25; Ali Ali/epa/Corbis: 24; Vince Bucci/Getty Images: 37; Fabrice Coffrini/ AFP/Getty Images: 20, 21; Johannes Eisele/AFP/ Getty Images: 33; Henghameh Fahimi/AFP/Getty Images: 34, 35; iStockphoto throughout: Ozgur Donmaz; iStockphoto/Syagci: 9; iStockphoto/ Stefan Baum: 13; iStockphoto/ javarman3: 29; Kaveh Kazemi/Corbis: 12; Atta Kenare/AFP/ Getty Images: Title page, 14, 18–19, 26–27; Peter Macdiarmid/Getty Images: 39; Win McNamee/Getty Images: 41; Mehdi Marizad/AFP/Getty Images: 6–7; Bruno Morandi/Getty Images: 42–43; Morteza Nikoubazi/Reuters/Corbis: 17, 23; Shutterstock Images throughout: Nik Nikiz; Javarman; c.; oriontrail; Francesco81; Fotoline; dusan964; Gememacom; Picsfive; Stephanie Pilick/epa/Corbis: 30; Mario de Renzis/epa/Corbis: 3; Reza/ Reportage/Getty Images: 11; Michel Setboun/Corbis: 10; Mohsen Shandiz/Corbis: 15; David Turnley/Corbis: 28; Zanan Magazine: 36